SAGITTAL SECTION

FIELD TRANSLATION SERIES 3

Miroslav Holub

SAGITTAL SECTION
POEMS NEW AND SELECTED

Translated by Stuart Friebert
and Dana Hábová

Foreword by Lewis Thomas

FIELD Translation Series 3

Grateful acknowledgement is made to the magazines FIELD, HAWAII REVIEW, POETRY NOW, WEST BRANCH, MALAHAT REVIEW, DURAK, HELIX, ONTARIO REVIEW, and THE NEW DIRECTIONS ANTHOLOGY Vol. #37, which published many of these translations. Some of these poems appeared in much different versions in the following books: "The Corporal Who Killed Archimedes," "Annunciation," and "Two" in ALTHOUGH (Jonathan Cape. London 1971); "Brief Thoughts On Cats Growing On Trees," "Brief Thoughts On Gargoyles," "Brief Thoughts On An Old Woman With A Cart," "Brief Thoughts On Eyes," "Brief Thoughts On Floods," "Brief Thoughts On Killing The Christmas Carp," "Dinner," "Daedalus" in NOTES OF A CLAY PIGEON (Secker & Warburg. London 1977); "The Fly," "Discobolus," "Man Cursing The Sea," "A Helping Hand," "Prince Hamlet's Milk Tooth" in SELECTED POEMS (Penguin. 1967).

Publication of this book was made possible through a grant from the Ohio Arts Council.

Library of Congress Cataloging in Publication Data
    Holub, Miroslav (translated by Stuart Friebert and Dana Hábová)
        SAGITTAL SECTION
        (The FIELD Translation Series; v. 3)
LC: 79-92784
ISBN: 0-932440-04-5
        0-932440-05-3 (paperback)

FOREWORD

Although scientists and poets appear from a certain distance to be two totally different sorts of professionals, engaged in occupations bearing no relation to each other, even seeming to be adversaries in the way they look at the world and in the rewards they seek from their work, it is not so. In real life, observed close up, they are engaged in the same kind of game. What they are looking for and sometimes, when they are good at their jobs, finding, are the points of connection between things in the world which seem to most people unconnected. They live out their lives in puzzlement and wonder, and when they are sufficiently skilled and lucky they achieve that most satisfying of all sensations available to the human mind: surprise. To be able to use one's own brain to generate one's own astonishment at the connectedness of things in the world is not an ordinary accomplishment; not many poets succeed in this, nor many scientists, but this is what they are up to, trying for.

Miroslav Holub is both kinds of professional, good at both approaches. His poetry is in this book, filled with jolting surprises and the suddenly visible evidences of unexpected relationships. His science is recorded elsewhere, in an extensive bibliography of technical papers and monographs dealing with lymphocytes and the strange capacity of these cells to recognize and remember the most precise details of an infinite number of chemical odds and ends in the confusing environment of living tissues, keeping things straight.

How Holub has managed to remain so active and productive in both his occupations, and to move from point to point with such sureness and obvious pleasure, is beyond me. Anyway, he does, and even if this single case does not establish my contention that poetry and science are the same enterprise, he does at least prove, conclusively, that they are not incompatible, and that, these days, is no small accomplishment.

LEWIS THOMAS

CONTENTS

III. *The Head*

IV. *Prolonged Reflections*

I

THE HAND

MAN CURSING THE SEA

Someone
just climbed to the top of the cliffs
and began to curse the sea.

Dumb water, stupid pregnant water,
slow, slimy copy of the sky,
you peddler between sun and moon,
pettifogging pawnbroker of shells,
soluble, loud-mouthed bull,
fertilizing the rocks with your blood,
suicidal sword
dashed to bits on the headland,
hydra, hydrolizing the night,
breathing salty clouds of silence,
spreading jelly wings
in vain, in vain,
gorgon, devouring its own body,

water, you absurd flat skull of water—

13

And so he cursed the sea for a spell,
it licked his footprints in the sand
like a wounded dog.

And then he came down
and patted
the tiny immense stormy mirror of the sea.

There you go, water, he said,
and went his way.

GEESE

Waddling along in a file
between lawns and crosses,
seeking the white god.

Week after week
one after another disappears
and white feathers
whirl in the kitchen.

The rest come
all the way back
and escort the empty place
waddling among them.

Week after week
each of them believes
in a last gasp,
this time for sure
our goose earth will change:

the waddling resurrection
in the feather heaven range.

DEATH OF A SPARROW

The death of a sparrow
is quite tiny,
        gray,
little wire
        claws.

And the dust
at the end of hopping
        calls,
        right now,
And the empty air
shuts its eyes and
        calls.

Mummy does all the
feeble chirping before nightfall
and
          calls,
the shadow flies away
and
          calls,

—No, we won't stay here,
the setting sun
          yells,
—Hurry, the rot's coming,
all the smoothness in the world
          begs and begs
          —Away!

Only
it's impossible
at the moment.

ON THE DOG ANGEL

False tears of light on macadam.
Maybe he was thinking of a bitch
or remembering a bone—
knives of evil-eyed wheels
caught and cut and crushed—

his jaw's dislocated, he
crawls off, yelps—no!
yelps, falls, whimpers
and lies still.

People around
see:
the dog angel,
shaggy and black
with muddy wings
and the huge pain
spreading its halo
over the puddles.

Darkness
wrings its hands
over the body and sound
columns to the sky.
They drag him
out of the way.

Just a rag,
a graveyard rag,
nothing more.

The angel's
on the roof,
sniffing the chimney,
gnawing the bones of shooting stars.

AUTUMN

And it is all over.

No more sweetpeas,
no more wide-eyed bunnies
dropping from the sky.

Only
a reddish boniness
under the sun of hoarfrost,
a thievish fog,
an insipid solution of love,
                    hate
                    and crowing.

But next year
larches will try
to make the land full of larches again
and larks will try
to make the land full of larks.

And thrushes will try
to make all the trees sing,
and goldfinches will try
to make all the grass golden,

and burying beetles
with their creaky love will try
to make all the corpses
rise from the dead,

Amen.

A HAND

We gave a hand to grass—
     and here is grain.
We gave a hand to fire,
     and here is a rocket.

Slowly,
hesitating,
we give a hand
to people—
     to some people.

GEOLOGY OF MAN

Some sort of
natural common
sense.

Some sort of
elementary value
of life.

Some sort of
goodness
of heart
or liver
or whatever.

These depths are in sand.

It takes just
one nasty wind,
one gulp of schnapps,
one drop of superstition
                from granny

and the flood is here.

Goodness
means mountain-making.

Without the magnetic
superimposed layer of necessity,
not a chip of sense
will show up.

Nothing but
eternal hemorrhage
stiffens on edges
into basalts and granites.

Man's
a job
for two million years.

THE DAM

Water
crowned.

Water grows, swallowing
the road and its shadows,
the house and its azure,
the slate and its ABC.

There are no more warm dens.
The earth is made of concrete.
Cranes have eviscerated the sky.

Centuries rush over the ridge now.

And not just on memories
        —on high voltage,
not on teardrops
        —on drum armature,
not on words
        —on thunder

we live.

A step aside and the alarm rings,
a step backward opens the abyss,
a tremor explodes.

Deep down
fish swim in cathedrals.

And every one of us
is called by name.

ACHILLES AND THE TORTOISE

> "*Achilles will never catch the tortoise*"
> —Zeno of Ellea

In the satin shade of an olive tree
Zeno shakes his head.

> For Achilles sinks in exhaustion
> like a dog chasing its tail,
> and the tortoise moves on
> to its burial in the sand,
> to hatch eggs,
> to drop dead,
> to be born,
> to swim over the Hellespont,
> to chew a primrose.

27

Zeno shakes his head.

> For Achilles will hardly run a thousand
>   meters
> and the tortoise
> crawls
> forever.

In the satin shade of an olive tree,
shaking his head,
Zeno dies.

> Achilles
> in his golden shin-guards,
> splendid and celebrated,
> gets up and readies himself
> for the last battle.

> But
> what is the name
> of the tortoise?

THE FLY

She sat on the willow bark
watching
part of the battle of Crécy,
the shrieks,
the moans,
the wails,
the trampling and tumbling.

During the fourteenth charge
of the French cavalry
she mated
with a brown-eyed male fly
from Vadincourt.

She rubbed her legs together
sitting on a disemboweled horse
meditating
on the immortality of flies.

Relieved she alighted
on the blue tongue
of the Duke of Clervaux.

When silence settled
and the whisper of decay
softly circled the bodies

and just
a few arms and legs
twitched under the trees,

she began to lay her eggs
on the single eye
of Johann Uhr,
the Royal Armorer.

And so it came to pass—
she was eaten by a swift
fleeing
from the fires of Estrés.

SOLDIER

Two hundred years ago
lying in the backyard,
his white coat trembling
in the dead calm.

The black shadow of oncoming
eternity
oozing underneath.

Whispering
Jesus,
Jesus . . .

And today still
that stone
in the rain
swells with blood
and the formidable
green
drugging
never forgetting grass,
mother grass
whispers
to daughter grass

Jesus . . .

STILL LIFE

Still Life with two little fish,
the Oxford dictionary and
Dopey the Dwarf in a yellow cap.

Days of reading from wall to wall.

Here and now
howling of fish behind glass.
Quivering of the dwarf
a cotton-wool Faustus wakes up in

And from the open sky
    Margaret's voice calling
Henry, Henry.

And then
hanging from the ceiling
some kind of thorn crown.

TWO

Over and over again
it's a headlong fall
from a crashing Astro-Jet
through the freezing void,
the clouds ripping clothes from limbs
and the deafening Earth coming closer
like a ferocious new formation,
a ball from a schizophrenic cannon.

And suddenly—touching the ground,
and suddenly—transposed,
and suddenly—thrust
into each other
we are
imprints of clay in clay
with crude oil spurting from us
through the riverbed of a home here, home there,
and dripping into the eyes
of vengeful angels
trapped in the doorpost.

And then, there is nothing wrong with us
but night,
and then, there is nothing wrong with us
but morning
and the forsaken glory of aviators
stripped of wings
in an unknown, strange land.

THE DANGERS OF NIGHT

The master bedroom; double bed; ceiling; bedside
    table; radio.
And out there the darkness supported by trees
under which a dark blue jaguar strolls.

The walls open and the double helix
of oneness
twists through the shadowy breath of the roof.

Perhaps galaxies. But more likely
the white of eyeballs in a suggestion of wind.

The enemy approaches: black image,
the image of self
in the mirror, sleep. Its hands
grow and touch each other
by fingertip.

Defend yourself, because in the morning,
in the light of mindless birds,
somebody else
will wake up.

ON THE ORIGIN OF FATHERHOOD

I know now. In the rains.
Under the ice, when each step
cracks with stars
and somebody watches from below.

In the evening, in the detonations of lights
of a distant city, on the edge of the planet.
In the attic of the house where I was born.
In the cellar of the house
where we used to put together from pieces of
    wood
something like a vertebra
and sternum, it may come in handy sometime.

In the nests of Faustuses and Iagos
and Desdemonas.

I know now. A little yolk, almost,
on the palm: I go up the staircase
and up the staircase, up and up

into the old living room.
But nobody would be there.
At the edge of my eye I caught a glimpse
of your little fingers
disappearing under the door.

II

BRIEF REFLECTIONS

BRIEF REFLECTION ON BRIEF REFLECTIONS

Brief reflections are indeed brief reflections. Accordingly, they are not poems, nor stories, nor editorials, nor columns. (Editors do not like nor's, insist on "poems" because of the short lines, and the reflections are distressed and the reviewers are annoyed.) Reflections are a deliberate sample of stereotypes which one nurses in one's nucleic acids, partly as remnants or engramata of the poems gone with the wind. If then reflections occasionally take form through something similar to verse, it is only because verse approximates speech more than prose does. Poetry can be written on school notebooks, on trees, on clouds and on the pavement of one-way streets, preferably. Brief reflections are written on newspaper only. After all, Ezra Pound said, literature is news which stays news.

The pike gave up the ghost,
but the teeth remained,
            says the wisdom of folklore on brief reflections about 100 years before they were written.

BRIEF REFLECTION ON LOGIC

The big problem is everything has
   its own logic. Everything you can
   think of, whatever falls on your head.
   Somebody will always add the logic.
   In your head or on it.

Even a cylinder makes sense, at least
   in that it's not a cube. Even a cleft
   makes sense, maybe just because
   it's not a big mountain.

A special logic must be assigned to cylinders
   that pretend to be cubes. And clefts
   that think they're big mountains.

The logic of these things is in fact that
   they strip other things of their meaning.

This reflection isn't abstract.

It's in view
   of recent history.

BRIEF REFLECTION ON IDENTITY

Day after day nothing repeats itself.
  Not rivers, not prophets, not goats.

And if the same today is the same tomorrow,
  it won't be that way, all things don't
  stay the same all the time. Because
  as soon as one thing changes, all other
  things change. Things are not alone,
  they closely depend on other things,

Or partly depend on them. So that,
  you know, one never knows . . .

Even the prophets are a part of this fixed
   relationship. So are words. So are goats,
   so is milk. So is blood.

So it's considerably difficult
   to recognize your own words, your own
   blood, your own prophet and your goat.

Considerably difficult. But again and again
   we try to, so that we don't get goats
   from prophets and blood from milk.

We pretend the identity of things,
   turning into our own doubles,
   marching slowly into the dark abyss of time.

BRIEF REFLECTION ON EYES

Goddesses, gods, fear and Twiggy all have very
   big eyes.
Some gods have such big eyes there's nothing
   left for the body
      and God equals his eye.
So the eye sees all, knows all and bestows gifts
   which would
      exist without the Eye, but are much better
      with the Eye.

Cyclopses, monster newts, stoolpigeons and angels
   of the apocalypse
      have very small eyes. But a lot of them.
One little eye in each keyhole.
Some angels, and others of the same rank, and
   here we don't mean exactly
      monster newts, have such small eyes there's
         no room in them
      for the smallest piece of man.
They lower their eyes to keep their secrets.

Behind our eyes the optic tracts reach the occipital
   lobes
      with their corresponding areas to the areas on
         the retina.
Behind very big eyes, there's nothing.
Behind very small eyes, the apocalypse.

BRIEF REFLECTION ON COLORS

Blue is certainly number four or even
   the vowel o, including birds and smoke
   of native Ithaka.

White is number one then, same as the vowel i,
   as long as it's out in the cold and not aligned.
   Then it also means the future of flowers,
   the past of books; blindness of the earth,
   opaque till now. Silence.

47

Black can be number nine, as long as it's not in the
    order
    of very refined numbers, even numbers fade
    if they're sophisticated; you too may be black
    sometimes, blackness can also occur in
    skull-like cliffs and caves; yes and in the order
    and anger of matter.

Red on the other hand is three, and as five
    it's lighter, more brown. The letter *a* is red
    like the open mouth of a small animal. Also,
    battle is red and Faust's pen and love
    in summer. And the fanfare of hope.

Therefore, we have an equation in four colors.
    4=1·9–5, likewise olive groves by the sea
    during the equinox and the period between
    two wars, which happens once a year at most.

No wonder the authorities don't love poetry and
    guards
    linger in the shadows where nobody can see
    how worried they are about the strict order of

Colors.

BRIEF REFLECTION ON CHARLEMAGNE

Outside, in front of the gate,
a bell hangs. Charlemagne, son of Pepin the Short,
had it put there. Those who've suffered injustice
can ring and Charlemagne interrupts being king,
receives them right away, listens to them
                          and metes out justice.

This happened in Eight Hundred.

The bell rang this year.
In the rain, more like
collapsing than dripping,
and lasting eleven hundred years,
drenched, seedy, sheepish,
in a clown's costume,
stood Charlemagne.

In broken Frankish, he demanded
a hearing.

49

BRIEF REFLECTION ON THE INSECT

The insect is really not built too well. It needs
    a better skeleton, a better respiratory system
      and
    a better central nervous system than this
      couple of
stupid knots. When improved along these
      lines,

    burying beetles can start public funeral
      services,
    scarabs rob banks, ants could be assigned
    to the space program and flies could supervise
    the whole world with big eyes, and make
      decisions,
    yes or no,
    good or bad,
    promote, punish.

The insect, safe from switching tails and DDT,
could reflect on the improvement of Man
who's really not built too well.

BRIEF REFLECTION ON COWS

We believe that a cow's mission in life is to be a
    cow.
That isn't really too difficult, when we're in the
    pasture.

The problems start on the way to the slaughter-
    house. Now we
        feel unknown fear, and the devils of the deep are
            tearing
        at our stomach, fat heart and pulpy emptiness of
            our brain.

Then we're kicking around, our head jerked by
     chains:
          the name
     different for all of us. Or standing in deep
          thought, which
     some may call resignation, sullenness or mental
          darkness.

Old wisdom is dumb—without any directions on
     how to
          escape from
     the sledge hammer and hatchet.

So we're sorry to be a cow, with so little knowl-
     edge about
          everything
     in this field. We want to be in somebody else's
          skin now.
     In a human being's skin. But this is just cow's
          thinking.

Even people often think—

BRIEF REFLECTION ON CATS GROWING IN TREES

Once upon a time, when moles still held their big
   conferences,
   and when they had better eyesight than they do
      now, the moles
   decided to find out just what was up there.

They elected a committee to supervise the project.
   This committee
   sent up a quick and clever mole who, when he
      left the motherland
   underground, spotted a bird sitting in a tree.

And so a theory was established; up there birds
   are growing on trees. But some moles
   considered this too simple. So they sent
   another mole up to learn more about birds
   growing on trees.

This time it was evening, and on the trees were
   squealing cats.
   Not birds, but squealing cats are growing on
      trees, announced
   this mole. An alternative cat-theory was there-
      fore established.

The two contradicting theories made it impossible
   for one neurotic
   member of the committee to fall asleep. He
      climbed up to see
   for himself. But it was night again, and pitch
      dark at that.

Nobody's right, announced the worthy mole.
   Birds and cats are
   optical illusions, which are evoked by the double
      refraction
   of light. Actually, he said, up there nothing is
      different
   from down here, only the earth is thinner and
      the roots on
   the other side are whispering something, really
      quietly.

They approved this theory.

Since then, moles have stayed underground with-
   out establishing
   any committees, and they don't believe in cats,

or believe just a little.

BRIEF REFLECTION ON THE BUTCHERING OF CARP

You take a mallet
and a knife
and hit
the right spot so it doesn't flop because
flopping causes complications and lowers profit.

The people watching squint their eyes, admire
   your skill,
reach for their money. And the paper is ready
for wrapping. And smoke rises from chimneys.
Christmas gapes out from the windows, spreads
   along the ground
and splashes in vats.

Such is the Law of Happiness.

But I wonder, is the carp really the right animal?

Because a much better animal would be one
which—stretched out—kept flat—pinned down—
fixed its blue eye
on the mallet, the knife, the money, the paper
the people and chimneys
and Christmas.

And quickly
said something. For example

These are my best days, these are my golden days.
or
Starry skies above me and moral law in me.
or
And it *is* turning.

Or at least
Hallelujah!

BRIEF REFLECTION ON AN OLD WOMAN
WITH A PUSHCART

Given: an old woman and a pushcart P.
Now you have a system of an old woman W and a
    pushcart P.

The system is moving from B the backyard to C the
    corner,
        from the corner C to R the rock, from the
        rock R
        to F the forest, from the forest F to H the
        horizon.

The horizon H is the point where vision ends
    and memory begins.

Nonetheless the system is moving
    at a constant rate V
    along a constant trajectory
    through a constant world and
    with a constant destiny
renewing its impulse and its sense from itself.

It's a relatively independent system;
in the regions from horizon to horizon
there's always one old woman with a pushcart.

So there's one geodesic unit once and for all.
    The unit of a journey there and back
    of autumn
    of our daily bread
    the unit of wind and low hanging sky
    of home in the distance
    of As we forgive others
    the unit of dusk
    of footprints and dust
    the unit of life's fulfillment amen.

BRIEF REFLECTION ON FLOODS

We were brought up to believe
     a flood occurs when
     water rises above every limit,
     covers wood and dale, hill and mountain,
     places of temporary and permanent resi-
        dence,

so that
     men, women, honored patriarchs,
     babes and sucklings, beasts of field and
        forest,
     creepycrawlies and heebee-jeebies
     huddle together on the last rocks
     sinking in the steely waves.

And only some kind of ark . . . and only
        some kind of Ararat . . . Who knows?
        Reports on the causes of floods vary
        strangely. History is a science
        founded on bad memory.

Floods of this nature should be taken lightly.

A real flood
        looks more like a puddle.
        Like a nearby swamp.
        Like a leaky washtub.
        Like silence.
        Like nothing.

A real flood is when bubbles
        come from the mouth
        and we think they're
        words.

BRIEF REFLECTION ON GARGOYLES

When the world was turning to stone
     cliffs grew out of diatoms, towns from sighs
          and
     imperatives from question marks.

When the world was turning to stone the angels
  living
     in mansard portals, behind cornices and
     steeples, stiffened into stale
     sulphuric devils. Gripping ledges with their
          tight claws
     they became gargoyles.

Now,
     they shoot off their mouths at passers-by,
     shouting:

     What are you staring at, you dodo!
     or:
     You are like dust, and to dust you shall return,
     or:
     Get outta here, stick to gravity!

When it rains, they pour out their hate in streams
   of water,
       shivering with delight and disrespect. At
          night they
       lick the ground with their pulpy tongues,
          making black
       white and vice versa.

As such, sometimes in spring, they're ashamed
       so they climb down, disguised as black cats
       and moonstruck marmots and fretfully
          criticize
       the gothic in general and gargoyles in
          particular.
       Then curious angels without portfolio
       descend from their heights and listen,
       gripping the ledge with their claws.
       And so they harden, turning
       to sulphuric stone.

This insures
       the continuity of gargoyles,
       the consistency of gothic fonts
       and the respect of passers-by, cats and
          marmots
       for gravity.

BRIEF REFLECTION ON DWARVES

In the far wide world
hordes of dwarves—
becoming by far the biggest dwarves
in the world.

Here comes Superlohengrin riding
on a superswan, to the singing
of supercigars that have mastered
the wedding march, superbly everlasting.
Geological layers of
dreams and words turned to gypsum,
dead sounds underfoot.

In the near world,
a hardly visible Snow White
shuffles on mice paths,
looking for the seven good old
dwarves

and her own
forlorn
milk tooth.

III

THE HEAD

IN THE GLASS JAR

The mountain's given birth to a mouse.
So that the name was not given, but saved for
    future use. So were
two hundred don't's,
sorry, I didn't mean to,
several ounces
of teachers and cops,

and the little wooden rocking horse.

He's stripped of tragedy.
He looks out of the formaldehyde and says,
next year I'll go to school
and my belly will be full
of other children.

We listen, ashamed of this
direction of blood.

NEWBORN BABY

With eyes like embers of an extraterrestrial
   civilization,
it occurs. Garbage in the wind.

> It asks:
> What about neurosecretion? Solved?
> Or this red shift of galaxies? Is it explained
>   yet?
> Have we got malignity under control?
> Or at least the theory of aspirin effects?
> And the particle wave problem?
> Laws of thermodynamics, number four?
> And what about this crappy mess here?

The newborn baby, plainly disappointed, becomes
   engrossed in itself.
Gradually, it's covered by fine hair, and at night,
   almost imperceptibly,
it whines.

But the pack moves away.

WISDOM

Never let poetry be a thicket,
not even paradisically, so it won't
devour the frightened fawn of sense.
>   And this is a story of wisdom
>   linked to the roots of life
> And therefore
>   of living in the dark,
>   blind.
> A boy still not bound by
>   the hemp handcuffs of speech.
> With only ten words on his tongue
>   like jingle bells.
> He's already wearing the iron shirt of disease,
>   it's heavier than an upright man could carry,
> In a white oblong, just like a glass mountain
>   from which all knights
>   fall down headlong—

There's nothing in the mind
that wasn't in life
    (Tuberculous inflammations
      of the brain membranes
      still occurred then.)
    On Christmas Eve, he got his first
      toys, a giraffe and a red car.
    In the corridor—far away from
      this land—stood the tree
      with tearful eyes.
There's nothing in life
that wasn't in the mind.

And the boy played among
    symptoms and in the blue valley
    of the temperature curve,
And between two lumbar punctures
    which are so much like
    crucifying,
He played with the giraffe and the red car
    which were
    all his crown jewels,
    all his Christmases
    and all his Punches in the world.
And when we asked if
    he wanted anything else,
He said with a feverish glance
    from beyond:

Nothing any more.
Wisdom's not in many things,
just in one

(At that time
meningitis still
killed.)

It was a very white Christmas,
        snow reached roots,
        frost reached heaven
And we could feel the glass mountain
        trembling under our hands.

And he kept on playing.

AT HOME

As if out of a last year's cobweb
she looked up from her creaky armchair:
"You look good, son."

And the wounds were healing,
we were children again
and there was no school.

And when things got too bad
and there was no night, no day,
there was no up, no down,
and we were losing our wind,

she would say
from the cobwebs,
you look good son.

And wounds were healing before her eyes,
even though

she was blind.

CROCHETING

With hooks delicate as the arms of stars
she twists the days and nights together
into an endless pullover.

She's the one
who'd dress the rocks in chenille,
draw the nautical miles of a ship at sea
through the soft tunnel of a sleeve
and wrap a stratospheric shawl
around meteors for warmth.

And yet
we walk around naked,
naked and cold,
sonny boys.

THE GARDEN OF OLD PEOPLE

Malignant growth of ivy.
And unkempt grass,
it makes no difference now.
Under the trees, the invasion
of the fruit-bearing Gothic.
Darkness set in, mythological
and toothless.

But Minotaurus beat it
through a hole in the fence.
Somewhere, Icaruses
got stuck in webs.

On a bright early morning
the bushes reveal
the unabashedly gray, impudent
frontal bone of fact.
Gaping without a word.

MA   MA

Lying and waiting. Can't sleep.
Doll faces on the ceiling.
Nobody coming but something coming.
Sits up and waits.
Nobody coming but it is here.
The wardrobe winking. Tears of the world
pushing into the eyes. Quietly crying,
reaching out her hand.
Sobbing mama, mama.

Silence. One flew east, one flew west . . .

Crying mama, mama, till it hurts,
but it keeps falling back like
gray crab apples of loneliness.
Choking mama mama
and lying down in whiteness,
the long polar snow all around.
Silence.

Nobody ever flew anywhere, in fact.

The painful spiral
of all miracles.

ma ma

Diagnosis: Bronchopneumonia,
multiple brain hemorrhages,
senile cachexia.
Earrings and ring put in trust.

ma . . . ma

CONVERSATION ABOUT POETRY
WITH A YOUNG ONE

Dead trunks straying above the watershed
and the ancient double candleholder
still holding the amazement of candles
and the mute fire
of irises.

There is so much we wanted, I wanted
to say,
and we said nothing at all.

CONVERSATION ABOUT POETRY
WITH A VENERABLE OLD GENTLEMAN

Fifteen billion brain cells,
fifteen billion waxen cells,
on the paper, ten words have dropped,
jolted by Maxwell's imp.

When reason comes back to us one day,
we will erase like hell,
turning the cells into a whirlwind.
And the words into a litany.

POEM TECHNOLOGY

It is
    a fuse,
which you set off
somewhere in the grass
or in a cave,
or in a third-rate
        saloon.

The flame darts
past stalks
and bewildered butterflies,
past startled stones
and drowsy mugs,
darts,

spreads a bit
        or shrinks
as pain in a surplus finger,
hisses, sizzles,
stops
        in a microscopic vertigo,

but at last,
at the very end,
        it blasts,
a bang from a cannon,

crumbs of words fly
            through the universe,
the walls of the day rumble

and although
the rock's not cracked,
at least somebody says—

    Shit, something happened.

ON DAEDALUS

Daedalus is puttering around his labyrinth.
The walls keep multiplying.
There's no escape.
Just wings.

But all around—so many Icaruses! The air is black
   with them.
In the towns, the fields, on the plateaus.
In airport lobbies / automatic
goodbyes / ;
In the Space Control Center / metempsychosis
by semiconductor / ;
On the playground / groups of student conscripts
class of 1960 / ;
In the museum / the blond beards
floating up / ;
On the ceiling / a fleck of rainbow
imagination / ;
In the marshes / baying in the night,
class of 1640 / ;
In the stone / the pleistocene finger,
pointing up / .

Time full of Icaruses.
Air full of Icaruses.
Spirit full of Icaruses.

Ten billion Icaruses
minus one.

And look, Daedalus still
hasn't invented
the wings.

EVENING IN A LAB

The white horse will not emerge from the lake
(of methyl green),
the flaming sheet will not appear
in the dark field condenser.
Pinned down by nine pounds of failure,
pinned down by half an inch of hope
sit and read,
sit as the quietest weaver
and weave and read,

where even verses break their necks,

when all the others have left.

Pinned down by eight barrels of failure,
pinned down by a quarter grain of hope,
sit as the quietest savage beast
and scratch and read.

The white horse will not emerge from the lake
(of methyl green),
the flaming sheet will not appear
in the dark field condenser.

Among cells and needles,
butts and dogs,
among stars,
there, where you wake,
there, where you go to sleep,
where it never was, never is, never mind—
search
and find.

SEVERAL VERY SMART PEOPLE

They spoke in pins
They were silent in needles.

The night leaned on
the tiny torn-up animal of the world
with her chilly hands.

Later, when they went home,
they kicked
            bread

from corner
            to corner.

IV

PROLONGED REFLECTIONS

ON THE NECESSITY OF TRUTH

I remember a man who was arguing at the movies. He was sitting in front of me, and at first he was quiet. Later, a short film was shown about the muskrat. The title was right, but the narrator kept saying "beaver." The man in front of me started to wriggle and grumble. After a while, when the honey-voiced narrator said "beaver" again, the man shot out: "It ain't no beaver, it's a muskrat, you . . ." The audience began to turn their heads and the narrator went on: "The fur of our beavers . . ." —"Damn, I said it was a muskrat!"—the man in front of me said hotly. He just couldn't stand it. He jumped up and waved his hands. He argued with those who wanted peace and quiet in the movie house, in spite of the untruth on the screen: "No . . . that's a muskrat . . ." —The narrator wasn't bothered; he was recorded on the film strip. But the man demanded the truth, he argued about the beaver with the automated voice. Then he got up and left, to scathing remarks from the vexed audience. He could not bear sitting there without the truth: it was a muskrat, not a beaver, and he left even though he'd paid for his ticket.

Nobody can live without the truth he knows. In one way or another. Nobody can tolerate crookneck squash being called turnips, or Sirius Aldebaran. The right name is the first step toward the truth which makes things things and us us. Which conjures away any peril of the nameless things, and which, finally, heals and feeds and helps us live. And such hairsplitting in natural history is on the one hand a phenomenon of essential human features, and an element of science on the other. Not even in the smallest things can one live without the truth. Let alone the great ones.

That's why I only have a good impression of the man in the movies. And of Socrates.

POETRY EVENING

To set up a so-called poetry evening, it's necessary to find a clubroom or some other adequate space, a chairperson or emcee who can speak in simple but sincere words, small quantities of music, or possibly even a poet. The latter can be replaced by an elocutionist in the event the poet is indisposed, absent or dead. In happy circumstances, poetry actually takes place; autographing books always does. The poetry doesn't so much consist of the intended recitation, but rather in circumstances unenvisaged and unplanned. It is something more like remembering the charm of those vacations when a cow would chase us than that a life-giving sun would shine on our heads.

To be specific: the youth center was located in a murky house in a blind alley on the edge of town, where nothing begins. There was a stroller on a step-platform, abandoned by the baby, who'd probably left to seek a better fortune. The club, however, had paneled-wood walls, was arrayed with sound equipment, and jumped with a proportionate number of young people in blue jeans, in such a sober state they contrasted delicately with the rich, manly howl coming from a nearby pub.

The center was built by the members. At the moment, the chairperson stated, Our team's building a nursery; attendants at the nursery could hardly be expected to assist in the construction. The chairperson alluded to some other local topics, and then, gradually, the evening got underway.

Some poetry was read, guitars were plucked, and chansons sung. The young people listened, not exactly reverently, but quietly. Then a problem arose. In the form of a very corpulent man of uncertain posture, who unwrapped himself from the darkness in the back and demanded an immediate discussion with leading members of 'this here thing.' The leading members respectfully proceeded to the backroom and the immediate discussion was conducted with considerable energy; the literature went on shakily on its frail legs, while the door convulsed with vernacular expressions of a heavy semantic caliber. The very corpulent man then returned in the opposite direction, proclaiming grumblingly in a variation on the last words allegedly uttered by a Czech folk hero before his execution: Just wait!

The program finally ended in an open forum of questions . . . Are there any more questions. . . . Anybody else . . . Following which four heavyweights including the former visitor invaded the room. One was in overalls, two in civilian clothes, one in a civilian, exuberantly flowered shirt. The relation of their weight to the mass of the young people present was totally in their favor, approximately two to one; as for the coiffures, it was vice versa. In the back room, the flowered man leaned against the counter, the man in overalls sat down, and the other two wobbled between. The young people and the participating cast gathered around and stared at poetry.

The basic issue was the fact that all the four men were firemen, while the young people in the club were not. On the contrary, they were engaged in useless activities. The first fireman, when passing by the club, was offended by the chairperson of the above-mentioned institution. How the chairperson managed to do that, while he was present at the poetry evening, remained a mystery.

Maybe it wasn't this guy here, reckoned the offended, but somebody from the club. Probably somebody emboldened by the verses.

And even if it wasn't nobody, declared the fireman in overalls, this here place shuts down because there's no sandbox.

But, the flowered man by the counter spoke, You, comrades, offended one of us and that's too bad.

Now you see our problems, one of the leading members whispered to the participating poet.

What'd ya say, vociferated one of the civilian firemen, Did you say you wanted to sock me?

Forget it buddy, you wouldn't want to repeat that. I'll kick you from here to Prague.

And you can stop right there, they didn't put that sandbox in and we already told them once, the first fireman maintained.

Comrades, you offended one of us and that's too bad, the flowered man repeated his message.

And you're not local anyway, the fireman in overalls cut to the quick.

I am, because I am the chairman here, the chairman claimed.

Discussion on this subject was sustained for about ten minutes.

But, concluded the flowered man at the counter, You, comrades, offended one of us, and that's too bad.

Then the fireman got up and left in the fashion of armor-clad knights of the medieval king, Przemysl Otakar, who had just crushed bloody foreigners of incomprehensible language and

detestable denomination. The marching, flow-
ered fireman turned to the poet and said, So
you're a poet? It sounded as if someone in a zoo
were addressing an exhibit: So you're a tapir?

The accosted had never heard this question
formulated with such pregnancy. He would
have liked to say no, but that wasn't feasible.
Besides, even a tapir is pretty, and often lives for
many years.

All summed up, it was an evening full of
poetry.

The plea hadn't concerned trivial matters.
The plea was metaphorically uplifted to super-
natural spheres; it reached a new profundity,
which the poet would certainly like to attain, if
he only knew how.

CONVERSATION ABOUT POETRY

This isn't quite the jolliest story you've heard. As a matter of fact, writing those can sometimes be rather sad.

Once, when I was deciding to enter poetry— and I wasn't half good at making my entrance— I held the opinion that this "department" embodies some core, something like a torch or credentials, passed down from one generation to the next. So I wrote to a prominent professor of a medical branch, who himself was a prominent, well-known poet. A conversation on the communicable core of the matter seemed to me most appropriate. I have since learned to avoid such impertinence. Before long, the professor replied in a very kind letter. At that time, people used to answer letters before too long, and the professor was one of those, for whom education and culture are an immediate cause of kindness. He was a very old professor and the letter was written in an exquisite style, accompanied by a beautiful signature. I believe I still have it somewhere. Only I don't know where.

We agreed on a personal visit at the professor's clinic. In about a month. I don't know what happened in that month.

But when I arrived in the metropolis and found the clinic, I was expected by a secretary. The conversation, she said, had been duly arranged, but she had to warn me that some serious difficulties had taken place. Difficulties of a medical nature. Nevertheless, I couldn't conceive of leaving. On the contrary, I had to carry out the visit, as the professor was expecting it. In fact, he was very much expecting it. Only she had to warn me . . .

Then I entered his study. More precisely, his study somehow sucked me in, and the soundproof door closed behind me. The professor was sitting erect and tense, absorbed by his own shadow against the window. He made a greeting gesture. He had the appearance of a man who'd been existing in that moment for some time. In order to make conversation, I narrated my anamnesis, and added a few halting statements on poetry. Statements on poetry usually limp. He nodded in a kind way, but didn't utter a word. I braced myself for a direct question, something on the relationship between medicine and poetry, which question I've never heard answered, although ever since I've answered it, about 892 times.

The professor inhaled deeply and with extreme care uttered several amalgamated vocals, terminated by a groaning rrr. The silence exploded; a rather horrible silence. I gathered he couldn't talk, but didn't know it yet. I gathered he was talking about poetry, and that he wanted to talk about it for the first time since the stroke that had caused his condition. I gathered my reaction was responsible for more than the logical destiny of the topic.

And so I tried to guess what sentence he'd meant to pronounce, and to continue with its idea. I said something like . . . yes, however, maybe both things spring from the same will to help, limited by learned rules, but free in the choice of specific application . . .

The professor said many many more amalgamated vocals and several r's and l's.

I said something about the unity of science and literature, and about the separation of science and literature in the period of the "third science," which was indemonstrable in terms of the senses . . .

Vocals. Rrrrr-l.

And so we communed. For twenty minutes maybe. Maybe for a quarter of our lives. Then we said goodbye. That could be estimated quite accurately. I already believed I understood everything. I was glad that at least by my terminal phrases he seemed assured that we'd really communicated things we had in mind. That it was a successful conversation.

Later, I saw that it had really been a successful conversation, touching the core of the matter. That it was in fact one of the most accurate conversations achieved by two individuals on the essence of so-called poetry. For it's the essence of poetry that, in making conversation, it does not speak. Making conversation of itself, it leads somewhere else; to certain rescue and preservation, while disregarding words and non-words. And directed elsewhere, it is confident of its own failure. And this confidence itself is full of hope.

It's the essence of poetry that always it does *not yet exist*. But it will.

It's not the jolliest story. Just slightly jolly. Because the curve of jollity penetrates rather deeply into sadness.

MEETING EZRA POUND

I don't know what came first, poets or festivals.

Nevertheless, it was a festival that caused me to meet Ezra Pound.

They seated him in a chair on a square in Spoleto and pushed me towards him. He took the hand I extended and looked with those light blue eyes right through my head, way off into the distance. That was all. He didn't move after that. He didn't let go of my hand, he forgot the eyes. It was a lasting grip, like a gesture of a statue. His hand was icy and stony. It was impossible to get away.

I said something. The sparrows chirruped. A spider was crawling on the wall, tasting the stone with its forelegs. A spider understanding the language of a stone.

A freight train was passing through the tunnel of my head. A flagman in blue overalls waved gloomily from the last car.

It is interesting how long it takes for a freight train like that to pass by.

Then they parted us.

My hand was cold too, as if I'd touched the Milky Way.

So that a freight train without a schedule exists. So that a spider on a stone exists. So that a hand alone and a hand per se exists. So that a meeting without meeting exists and a person without a person. So that a tunnel exists—a whole network of tunnels, empty and dark, interconnecting the living matter which is called poetry at festivals.

So that I may have met Ezra Pound, only I sort of did not exist in that moment.

THE DOG THAT WANTED TO RETURN

Destinies of experimental dogs are not obvious until the moment they're delivered to the site of the experiments. They arrive in a closed station wagon, filled with dog-dread and mystery formulated by philosophers in such questions as, Where do I come from? Where am I going? Canines formulate these questions by leaving puddles and whining.

At the experiment site, the dogs are enclosed in cages according to their races and natures. The dog-keeper, assisted by a hose, is the sun of their days; he serves the indefinite dog stew, their sole suitable escapade. The rest consists of howling, attempts to jump three meters high, pass through the wire netting sparrows can penetrate, mate with dogs of the same sex, murder dogs of smaller size, and defend their cages by barking hysterically. For such is the natural disposition of a dog. Even the cages have to be watched over, natural disposition dictates.

A dog is selected for experiments if for two weeks he has manifested a healthy condition, and if his weight is satisfactory. He is then taken on a leash by the keeper. The joy in his tail is immense, and all co-dogs envy him with all their hearts. The dog on the leash thinks it's time for his walk with his master again. This walk, however, is very long. It is never terminated and therefore never repeated.

Once though a small spotted dog with a white chest and a bell collar slipped out. He ran away. He was fleeing. For such is the natural disposition: to flee a place of fear, of whining and desperation.

He was running in ever-increasing circles around the cages. The circles were irregular, depending on how he was chased. He was chased by the keeper. He was chased by fences. He was chased by buildings. He was chased by trees and bushes. He was chased by the grass and flowers. He kept running and he realized he feared fences and buildings and trees and flowers. And while fleeing and fearing, he discovered he even feared his keeper, although the man had been the sun of his days. And that is why he didn't let anybody catch him. And that is why he stopped being an experimental dog and became a dog. A dog-as-such.

Such is the natural disposition of things: having lost predetermination, we lose our attributes.

The small spotted dog-as-such crawled through the fence, and set out into the streets. Yet, there was not one house, car, or stone he recognized. He met the local dogs accompanied by their masters. He did not recognize them either. Yessir, I'm from far away, from the Moravian border, he said to himself, trying to explain it, if a dog-as-such can say anything at all. He didn't recognize, he didn't belong, didn't belong to the streets, dogs, days or nights. Such a dog is dog that does not belong.

Not from hunger, but from not-belonging this dog realized he had to go back. He abandoned the windy breezes of the streets and corners, he crawled through the fence, he recognized trees that had chased him, he felt the scent of dog-fright and predetermination, he heard the hysterical barking of those who had guarded their cages from the invasion from Aldebaran, he recognized the station wagon and the stew bucket, and not seeing any keeper he approached the cages, welcomed by the raging hatred of co-dogs. He was quiet, for a dog without an attribute has neither a voice of advice nor a voice of warning. He crept toward his cage and tried to get in, he tried to pass through the wire netting penetrated by sparrows. He tried with his right paw and with his left. He tried to dig, he tried to jump three meters high. He tried it from all sides and he tried in vain. Such is the natural disposition of things: it's impossible to reenter one's destiny.

So he spent the night under old rabbit hutches, in the closest proximity to his cage, lay down and rolled into a ball-as-such.

In the morning, he avoided the keeper. At dusk, he returned to his cage. His flight became a circular pilgrimage from the non-existence of freedom to the indubitable existence of the cage. For such is the natural disposition of things: even though it's impossible to go back, it's imperative to keep going back.

Moreover, belonging is contained in a dog's mind, while being-as-such is not contained in it.

This dog belongs to this cage and this fear.

Nights, when villainous cats lurk behind the bushes, and the aggressive stomping of rabbits can be heard, the eyes of the small dog under the rabbit hutch radiate the red, reflected light of lamps and planets, and the canine supernatural life: endlessly, until on his circular pilgrimage an unknown car hits him, and he becomes an experimental dog angel, an angel which will receive a leash and be weighed and selected for the experiment on the subject of the Influence of Eternity on the Natural Disposition of a Dog.

V

HEART FAILURE

ANNUNCIATION

It could be the erratic neighing of the night
outside, below the window,
when fire settles to sleep.
It could be the horns of Jericho,
it could be the choir hymn
    of hunchbacks underneath the snow,
it could be the oak speaking to willows, ·
it could be the chiffchaff hatching
    under the owl's wing.
It could be the archangel's decision,
and it could be the salamander's ominous prophecy.
It could be the weeping of our only love.

111

But the official slumped over his desk
turned to us and said:
Let us hearken: You must hearken.
You are expected to hearken.
Hearken more boldly,
boldly hearken more,
hearken, heark, he hearketh,
they hearken, more boldly,
we more boldly hearken,
hea rk en,
HEAR K EN,
HeaR k En Hear—
So we didn't hear a thing.

TEACHER

The Earth is turning,
    says the pupil.
No, the Earth is turning,
    says the teacher.

Thy leaf has perish'd in the green,
    says the pupil.
No, Thy leaf has perish'd in the green,
    says the teacher.

Two and two is four,
    says the pupil.
Two and two is four,
    the teacher corrects him.

Because the teacher knows better.

SUPPER

You must eat all your soup, that's how you get
strong.
Eat that soupie, stop playing with it!
Or else you'll be weak and you won't grow up.
And that'll be your fault.
If it comes to that, towns and nations are to blame
when they don't grow up.
I blame small towns for not becoming cities. Their
tough luck.
I blame little nations for not growing powerful.
Their tough luck.
Accuso le piccole nazioni . . .
Ich beschuldige die kleinen Nationen . . .
J'accuse les petites nations . . .
So bolt that soup, before it turns to ice!

PRINCE HAMLET'S MILK TOOTH

His tooth fell out milky as
    a dandelion
and everything began to fall,
    as if a rosary had broken,
    or the string of time had snapped,
and it was downhill all the way;
round the corner the hearse driver gets up from
    supper,
his blind horse leading him, jolting along.
Hamlet, we're on our way.

No time now except hurry—
    learn to add and multiply,
    learn to cheat, whisper answers,
    smoke and make love,
    lay in stocks of permanganate
    and naphthalene,
there won't be any more.
And we're on our way, Hamlet.

At dusk you hear the drunken Danes making a
    racket
    and the pollinated flowers trampling around,
at dawn the typewriters tap out
    piles of loyalty checks
    with skeleton fingers,
at noon the paper tigers roar
    and committees count off races,
    what will be left for seed
    when it's all over?
Hamlet, we're on our way.

But we'll put a bird on our heads
    instead of a soldier's cap, won't we?
We'll walk through the park

    and in the shadow of a red rock
('come in under the shadow of this red rock')
    we'll learn
    to think it over
    in a small way,
    the way moss grows,
    the way sponges soak up water,
or we'll take a walk
    five minutes out of town,
    grow smaller and smaller,
    a pacemaker over our hearts,
    tuned to an easy rhythm

so the wolf has eaten, and the goat's still there,
we'll take the oath a little
    and lie a little,
    because not lying's in short supply,
brave lads, salt of the earth,
with our muddled hopes
one fine day
    we'll damn well prove our salt,
Hamlet.

And keep that tooth of yours.
That's all there is.

WHALING

There is a shortage of whales in some cities.
And yet, the whaling fleet cruises the streets.
A huge fleet in such a small town.
Or at least a harpoon creeps
from one sidewalk to the other,
and searches . . . and finds.
The house is pierced and in minute jerks
a weird creature quivers.
Minute blood soaks into the wall.

118

And that is the Old Testament plot,
the elementary drama,
the essential event,
to be pierced and dragged away,
between textbooks and copybooks,
        between algae and halibut,
between mummy's cups and pictures,
        between seaweed and cat's-paws,
between slippers and webs in the corner,
        between Morning star and Evening star,
to be pierced and dragged to glorify
the gods of piercing and dragging,
to be pierced and dragged to eternity,
in the stifling inner bellowing of blood,
wanting to remain and with convulsing claws
clutching the water drop on the tap,
reflections in the window pane,
the first baby hairs
        and fins.

But there is nothing but waves, waves, waves
and the undoing
of that nameless other shore,
with nothing good or bad,
just the arcuation of bones,
The scraping of plaster under which come to light
still older and older medieval frescoes,
The sloughing of skins under which stands out
the sliminess of the fetus just conceived.

And the maledictory unison of pipes is heard,
the music of whalers,
the fugue towering over one place
like an obelisk of the last breath
behind the curtains.

Nobody ever wrote
Antigone of whales, Electra of whales,
Hamlet of whales, Godot of whales,
Snow White of whales, not even
one flew over the whale's nest,

although the whale as such
is a sort of a metaphor.

Metaphors die out
in a situation which is a metaphor.
And whales die out
in a situation which is a killer whale.

THE CORPORAL WHO KILLED
ARCHIMEDES

With one bold stroke
he killed the circle, tangent
and point of intersection
in infinity.

On penalty
of quartering
he banned numbers
from three up.

Now in Syracuse
he leads a school of philosophers,
for another thousand years
squats on his halberd
and writes:

one   two
one   two
one   two
one   two

DISCOBOLUS

But
before his last throw
someone whispered from behind
    —Just a minute,
    we've got to talk this over—
    purely as a matter of form,
    —You don't know the set-up,
buddy,

    OK, so you've got
    some initiative, but
    don't you get it

    —We've got to insist on
    total agreement
    for every throw,

he felt
the soft Sudanese reed
wind around his wrist,
he wanted to yell
but his mouth
was suddenly full
of the cotton candy of the night sky,

his muscles bulged
like Thessalien granite,
yet
there was really no point to it,
    —Keep moving,
    someone said,
    get out of the way, will you,

    Demosthenes'
    turn now,
and Demosthenes
took a grain of sand from under his tongue
and neatly
flicked it in his eye,

    —Hurrah, one more
    world record,
    they shouted;

beside himself, in a fury, stripped of his name,
Discobolus
swung down from
his knees again
but he was
stone by now
and saw
just a single
huge grain of sand
from horizon to horizon.

So he just stood there.

And round the corner
the first school buses
led
by the best pedagogues
who referred mostly
to the play of shoulders,
the great big human heart
and the proud step forward
on the way to eternity.

SOCRATES

A suspicious character
with a saddle nose,
the eyes of a debauchée,
a bum corrupting the young,
despising communal gods,
dangerous by his uselessness
and he only drank hemlock.

He should have been covered by wet rags,
he should have been worked over by experts,
he should have lost his nails
    him and his final end in life.

He should have been stabbed by searchlights,
scanned by electric shocks,
    him and his worrying about the soul.

He should have got the chair,
he should have been put to the wall,
    him and his notions of goodness.

He should have been shot on the run,
    him and his bull's eye.

In fact
many times
a Socrates,
good, bad,
reliable, unreliable,
acceptable, unacceptable,
was nailed to the door like a bat

just because nails are
in better supply than
Platonic dialogues.

Yesterday, I think
I saw Socrates, talking in the agora,
smiling.

GALILEO GALILEI

Flies licking the fish eyes of the saints.

    I, Galileo Galilei,
    Florentine, at seventy years of age,
    kneeling in front of your highnesses . . .

The trampling of the ages stops.
Holy manna
trickles down the fur of time and space,
the cosmic hen head
with its beak smashes the teeth of pegged-out stars,
hallelujah, hallelujah . . .

    I, Galileo Galilei,
    in the state of being sentenced,
    solemnly swear . . .

The Earth shudders.
The Sun torn from its roots
falls with a scream,
the Universe shrinks into Halloween candles
astronomers grow blind . . .

I, Galileo Galilei,
swear
that I have always believed,
that I believe now
and with God's help I shall always
    believe . . .

dead tired men at microscopes
ask—what now,
children at their desks get up,
ABC books bleed,
history-bearers put down their panniers,
half-ways,
half-deeds,
half-truths,
stuck like a bone in a throat . . .

    . . . all that is proclaimed, recognized and
        taught
    by the Holy catholic, apostolic, Roman
        Church . . .

Silence.
The Earth was rendered,
the Sun was rendered,
dreams freeze in veins.

He, Galileo Galilei,
Florentine, at seventy years of age . . .

    I, Galileo Galilei,
    in a shirt, in Minerva's church,
    carrying the weight of the world
    on my spidery legs,
    I Galileo Galilei,

    whispering
    into my beard,
    just for children, bearers, the Sun—
    whispering
    I say in the end . . .

And the Earth
really does
turn.

HOMER

Seven cities quarrel about his crib:
Smyrna, Xios, Kolophon,
Ithake, Pylos, Argos,
Athenai.

He trots like a little ram
in the marine pastures,
unseen, hasn't been buried,
can't be dug up,
without a shadow.

130

Didn't he have difficulties
with the government?
Didn't he drink? Wasn't he
bugged, at least when singing?
Didn't he love fox terriers, chicks,
boys?

How much better the Iliad would be,
if Agamemnon had his traits
and Helen's biology would refer
to historical realities.

How much better the Odyssey would be,
if he had two heads
and one leg
and one wife
shared with his publisher.

He didn't care, somehow,
in his blindness.
So he's stuck
in literary history
as a warning example
of the author so unsuccessful
he didn't even exist.

HEART FAILURE

The airport is closed.
The plane circles round like
a fixed idea
over the closed city,
over porters, over dogs,
over troughs, over not-for-sale window-dressing,
over mailmen, roosters, and hens,
over brewers and tiny springs.
The airport is closed.

Tiny Spring, give water
to my little Rooster:
He's lying in the yard
with his feet up—
I'm scared he'll die.

Water dripping from faucets,
the city tumbling down.
There are no matches
for the synthesis of a star.
Somebody has stolen Charon's paddle,
it's strictly forbidden to use the ferry,
the Last Judgment's postponed,
come next week,
spring will be pink
as Aphrodite's ass.
Water dripping from faucets.

Miss Seamstress, give a scarf
to the tiny Spring, it will
give water to my little Rooster:
He's lying in the yard
with his feet up—
I'm scared he'll die.

The museum is bulging.
Tiny letters crawl out
like water fleas,
and even the trees scratch themselves.
Drowned dictionaries float.
On top a golden inscription
—Curse Those Who Hate Art—

Down below, the split, tinkered-up
museum is bulging.

   Mister Shoemaker, give shoes
   to Miss Seamstress,
   Seamstress will give a scarf to tiny Spring,
   tiny Spring will give water
   to my little Rooster:
   He's lying in the yard
   with his feet up—
   I'm scared he'll die.

Tender madness of ashes
in the lungs of the streets.
Black blood of poetry
in the veins of the pavement.
Street cleaners fall behind in their work.
In the madding crowd
somebody knelt down;
So what, they say,
so what, and they're right.
Tender madness of ashes.

Good Swine, give your bristles
to Mister Shoemaker,
Shoemaker will give shoes to Seamstress,
Seamstress will give a scarf to tiny Spring,

134

tiny Spring will give water
to my little Rooster:
He's lying in the yard
with his feet up—
I'm scared he'll die.

To bear at least one destiny, darling.
You are here but at the same time
you're crying far away.
Home is like a closed
metal rose and dead loves
knock on the roof with little parched fists.

And the one and only tear circles round
as the thirteenth planet,
transparent, uninhabited,
absolutely useless.
To bear at least one destiny.

Mister Brewer, give the Swine some draff,
Swine will give her bristle to Shoemaker,
Shoemaker will give shoes to Seamstress,
Seamstress will give a scarf to the tiny Spring,
Spring will give water to—

—Damn it, I can't remember to what . . .
The empty barrels of heaven rumble

right over our heads,
at night deep down inside
lions roar in thimbles.

and in the cracking of vertebrae
and the yelling of arteries
somebody is singing

    —tiny Spring, give water,
    in the yard, in the yard,
    in the yard, in the yard,

somebody is singing on and on
just like that—

Probably the little rooster.

PHILOSOPHY OF FALL

Fingers of the autumn sun
fiddle with yellow foliage
outside. The window reflects
a book and a silhouette
and a silhouette, a halo of hair,
this year we are
immersed in history
like a web in light.

I'm asking whether the existing
lack of genius
is caused by the elimination
of tertiary stages of syphilis.

Some God's spider
hovering above you, above me,
and above the Alka Seltzer.

ON THE ORIGIN OF THE CONTRARY

As if the sky broke up,
only it was just two palms of a hand.

It flapped its wings for a while,
but the palms closed
a little more. The wings got stuck.
It kicked its feet, but the palms
closed, one of its feet broke off.

Each time it moved something,
the palms closed and something broke off.
So it grew torpid. It could be
catalepsy.

But it could be the creeping realization
that blue sky did not exist any more.
                    On the contrary.
That there is no meadow with a flower
here and there.
                    On the contrary.
That there is nothing irresistible any more.
                    On the contrary.
That there is no glucosis,
            no droning,
            no time,
                    On the contrary.

And thus will it be. Until
someone gets bored. By that life,
that death, or that tickling in the palm.

ON THE ORIGIN OF LEGAL POWER

This time,
when houses sit on eggs
of the little painted easter death
and the symphony orchestra
is dug in behind the bushes,

when bassoons and trombones
loom up on the road,
asking for alms bigger than
the live weight of the body,

and he, listening to
the inner unison we used to know by heart,
to the tempest-in-the-teapot,
to his in-spite-of-all-that,
does not recognize the big city
because of the fast little flame,
does realise the fatigue of the mountain mass
face to face with a falling stone,

and
at least this time,
when asked, replies

Yes, I can.
And goes
the way of the flute.

THE LAST JUDGMENT

A fully automatic
washing machine is on—
washing, squeezing out, spinning dry.
As if angels were chewing gum.
As if granite bore quartz.

Someone's cursing the sea,
but you can't hear it.
Goose feathers whirl in the kitchen.
Your little fingers disappear
under the door.
The Icarian games of flies cover
the flaws in the labyrinth.
You look good, son,
and it is a heart failure.

The washing machine runs.
The Lucullan feasts get in
and two ounces of granola fall out.
The reflections get in. Well-ordered
letters fall out. The whales get in
and numbered teeth swim out.
Memory gets in and out slip
traffic regulations.

White. The washing machine runs.

And who's going to pay the band?
And where will the firemen's ball take place?
And where could the flute still peep
in the frost? How to step over
the book's shadow?

White of washed soot.

The washing machine runs so that
Discobolus' hands are trembling.
The time of eternity is measured out
with a second precision.

Yes.
In the landscape of games
one must play on till the end.

In the landscape of muck
the way out is
the washing machine.
In the landscape of chaos
one-way streets
are a real relief.
In the landscape of extinction
precision is more than godliness.

In the white noise
I leave through a door
leading
to the same room.

THE FIELD TRANSLATION SERIES